Foreword

KU-441-589

What makes this book different from other introductions to management and leadership is that it is specifically tailored to clinical research and so directly relevant to you.

If you are new to management or have been in management for some years, and wonder whether what you are doing by instinct and common sense, makes the best sense, then this book is for you. What you will be is busy and I have aimed to write something that is easy to read, and of practical use.

Organisations are groups of people working together and so the primary focus of this book is on the 'people management' issues that you will need to engage with, in order to perform effectively in the rapidly changing, diverse and fast moving world that is clinical research today.

As a result of many years spent as a consultant, trainer and manager in a huge diversity of public and private sector organisations, I believe that becoming an effective manager is more than a matter of acquiring a set of skills and tools to do the job. My starting point is well expressed in the quote below and forms the guiding principle of this book.

"I believe that management is an art and possibly one of the most difficult ones. Mere technical command of the skills does not, however, produce ... a superb manager. It is that extra something that each of us brings from within ourselves that makes a difference – vision, judgement, awareness of the world around us, and responsiveness to that world, which leads to success. Managing is a matter of the mind and the character..."
Sir John Harvey–Jones, *Managing to Survive, London, Heineman,1993*

The Institute of Clinical Research

GARTNAVEL ROYAL HOSPITAL

GRH008854

Maria Henderson Library
Gartnavel Royal Hospital
Glasgow G12 0XH Scotland

The
Institute
of
Clinical
Research

raising standards
sharing knowledge
developing professionals

The leading organisation for clinical research professionals

Internationally recognised as the premier organisation for clinical research, respected as a key influencer, promoting knowledge and understanding by engaging the healthcare community and the general public.

Raising standards

The Institute's professional standards encourage our members to work to the highest standards, enhancing the standards of clinical research and maintaining the professional identity of members

The Institute recognises the academic achievement and clinical research experience by awarding designatory letters e.g. MICR to our members.

Sharing knowledge

The Institute offers a comprehensive range of Information Services and publications, including our journal Clinical Research focus, our publications, online resources, a resource centre and membership helpline.

Developing professionals

The Institute provides educational courses and training workshops, continuing professional development, academic qualifications and accreditation of training courses. All of these enhance the professional competence of our members.

For more information call +44 1628 899755
or visit www.icr-global.org

About the Author — Rachel Harrison

Rachel Harrison runs a company specialising in communications and management development for employees at all levels in an organisation.

She has a proven track record of training and consultancy work within the clinical research industry across Europe. This is in addition to a very extensive and diverse experience of training, research, writing and consultancy across the charity, arts, media, health and education sectors in the UK and abroad.

Rachel spent the first fifteen years of her professional life in education arts and media. This includes full time roles as a senior lecturer in performing arts and education adviser at the BBC. She brings to her work in the clinical research industry an experienced and informed understanding of how other organisations and industries manage and develop.

Acknowledgements

With thanks to Helen Cazalet, Martin Heaney, Gareth Hayes, Mirella Von Lindenfels, Jo Burmester, Jan Burnell and all those who took the time and trouble to speak to me about their experiences as managers in clinical research.

With th   Communication for source   evelopment p30.

LIBRARY

Learning
Resource Centre

Contents

Introduction

This book does not pretend to be an exhaustive exploration of management thinking. Instead, the book draws on some of the most useful and pragmatic of generic management thinking currently available. It supports this with examples and illustrations and case studies from your industry, on occasions, drawing from other industries. To preserve confidentiality, the quotes included from managers in practice have been left anonymous. An annotated bibliography at the end will point you in the right direction for useful further reading.

How to use this resource

Each chapter in this book can be read on its own and the main index will steer you to items of particular interest within each section. Chapters are cross-referenced throughout, so that you will be guided to other useful and relevant information elsewhere in the publication. Reading the book from cover to cover will give you a concise introduction to the skills and qualities needed to making a success of managing your staff, your time and your work.

What's in the resource?

What is management really all about? Chapter One, **The Art of Management,** explores management and leadership with quotes and thinking from academic management thinkers and from practitioners in your industry. It looks at the differences between management and leadership. It draws on current management theory to examine the point and purpose of management and to articulate the specific and key tasks you need to perform well in the role. The chapter finishes with an outline of the skills and qualities associated with effective management and refers you to the parts of the book that cover these in more detail.

Chapter Two, **How Do You Manage?** starts from the premise that there is no 'right' style of management, there is your style of management. The most effective managers are those who know themselves, their strengths and their limitations and who are prepared to critically review their practice.

It looks at the importance of self-organisation, at proactivity and at time and task management, providing you with the thinking and tools necessary to carry out a critical appraisal of your organisational skills. This chapter also gives practical guidelines on making meetings work, project management and effective decision-making. The final part focuses on your management style and uses one particular model, **Situational Leadership,** as a framework for considering different management approaches to getting the best from people. It also gives you a model for critically reviewing and developing your management approach and concludes with an exploration of the art of delegation.

The focus of Chapter Three, **Managing Performance,** is on how to make a success of line management and appraisal in ways which draw out the best performance from members of your team. It gives practical guidelines on these, with checklists and questions to ask when preparing for review and appraisal sessions. There is a section on managing performance and setting objectives, together with some useful frameworks for thinking about staff development and progression and how best to support this.

Chapter Four, **Managing People**, looks at what makes communication work and specifies the factors essential to building constructive and productive working relationships. The second section of the chapter asks why we work and explores just how differing motivations and values about work affect performance, the manager's task being to uncover and tap into the differing motivations of their workers in order to get the best performance from people. Section three looks at managing difficult behaviour and offers strategies for dealing with difficult behaviour and difficult communication. Working with conflict is examined in section four. There are examples of sources of workplace conflict together with strategies, guidelines and real life examples concerning preventing, anticipating and resolving conflict situations. This chapter concludes with a focus on the manager as coach and mentor.

Chapter Five, **Leading and Managing Teams**, provides a comprehensive introduction to what teams need in order to perform optimally. It offers extensive checklists, guidelines and questions to help you with team building and teamworking. There is an explanation of the life-cycle of teams and of your role as a team leader or manager at each of the stages in this cycle.

The final chapter, **Managing Change**, examines the causes and experiences of change in the workplace. It provides examples of different types of change in the clinical research industry, together with examples of how to work constructively with change. The chapter asks you to reflect on your personal reactions to change, it explores the different responses to change from the individuals you manage and concludes with guidelines on how best to steer the change process for yourself and your team.

Chapter One - The Art of Management

Who wants to be a manager?

A management post is a natural progression for most of us wanting to advance at work. The more expertise we develop within a specific discipline, the more likely it is that we will be 'rewarded' for this by promotion into management. The clinical research associate, with a year or two of experience in the field, is made 'study team leader', or will 'act up' into a management position in the hope that the new role will be made permanent.

We quickly learn that, while some of the skills and qualities we have developed in the course of work to date are also useful to management, there is a whole new set of skills that we must somehow learn while doing the job. Many of us take on and are expected to take on, management roles with little or zero training in management. Contrast this with the effort put into training for other disciplines.

For many of you, your role as a manager is squeezed into an already overflowing job description. Not only do you now have to do the work, you also have to manage others doing it. How to find time to do this is the perennial dilemma for most people in junior and middle management roles.

And what of the skills and qualities it takes to make all this work? It can feel as though we are expected to know how to manage by osmosis or telepathy. The management role can be a lonely one. Suddenly, we are no longer a part of a team in the same way. We carry a different set of responsibilities and may have to make decisions that others in the team are less than happy with. We are sandwiched between the expectations of our superiors and the expectations of our staff. It can be difficult to ask for help and advice in the belief that we somehow should 'know' what to do. We are beset with insecurities and fears about getting it 'wrong', not delivering the goods or being seen as unconfident and incompetent.

"I really felt as if I had to know all the answers and keep everybody happy all the time, I ended up thoroughly miserable until I realised that I did not have to be all things to all people."

"I take great pride in my work as a data manager and feel confident in the role, recently I was promoted to team leader, now I have to do my own job and manage other people doing theirs. I had no idea how complicated it would be, I was totally unprepared for having to deal with people like this and feel as though I don't have the first idea of how to relate to them."

The Institute of Clinical Research

The Good News: You know more than you think you do

Much of good practice in management is in fact common sense. The best place to start exercising that common sense is on yourself.

Those who make the best managers are people who have a well developed, realistic sense of their strengths and limitations. You cannot be all things to all people. You cannot be perfect and you cannot achieve everything. It really does not matter how many books you read or courses you attend, effective managerial practice starts with your ability to manage yourself. This involves taking a critical and honest look at your actions and reactions to people and events and at the way you manage time and tasks in the workplace.

It means recognising the situations that you manage less than well and creating constructive ways forward for dealing with these, using your strengths. *There is no right style of management,* there is your style of management, based on a considered assessment of your capabilities and what you do well as much as on a clear identification of those areas that need development.

You will learn by experience and it's OK to make mistakes.

Use your experience, with its mistakes as well as its successes as learning opportunities. Take the time to reflect on and critically appraise your actions and reactions.

What is management ?
The gurus say...
"Management work is more an art than a science, reliant on intuitive and non-explicit processes." **Mintzberg,** *Nature of Managerial Work*

"Management, above everything else is about people. It is about the accomplishment of ends and aims by the efforts of groups of people working together. The people and their individual hopes and skills are the greatest variable and the most important one." **Sir John Harvey-Jones**

Managers in clinical research say....
"It's the ability to be a good listener, to keep your eye on what's going on around you. There's lots of reading between the lines at the same time as keeping your eye on the ball."

"It's getting the balance between the needs of the team versus the needs of the business. Getting people to deliver without destroying them in the process."

"Pressure in terms of deadlines and productivity is huge, particularly in CRO environments, the thing that sometimes suffers is the real development of people."

"There are usually utilisation targets which are unrealistic especially when a lot of the people tasks of management you can't actually bill for."

Leadership v management: What's the difference?

The gurus say...

"Managers do things right, leaders do the right thing."   **Warren Bennis**

"The most effective leaders, political or corporate, empower others to act – and grow – in support of a course that both leaders and followers find worthy."
Tom Peters

"Leaders do not need to know all the answers. They do need to ask the right questions."   **Heifetz, R.A., Laurie, D. L.,** *The work of leadership, Harvard Business Review , Jan/Feb, 1997*

"Today's leaders have to be pragmatic and flexible to survive. Increasingly, this means being people rather than task-oriented. The 'great man' theory about leadership rarely applies, if teams are what make businesses run, then we have to look beyond individual leaders to groups of people with a variety of leadership skills."   **Robbert Sharrock,** *interviewed by Crainer, S., Key management Ideas, Prentice Hall, 3d ed.*

Managers in clinical research say...

"Straight-up management is about ensuring the people are doing what they are supposed to do. Leadership is about getting them to go on a journey with you somewhere."

"In CR, people are marked or rewarded for achievement of tasks or milestones, the task of the leader is to take them across the line."

There are many debates over the differences between the two roles. Current thinking recognises that there is a leadership component in many managerial roles. This is the aspect of your role, that involves giving direction, providing inspiration, becoming a role model to others, or leading by example.

As a team manager, people will look to you for clear and consistent direction. This leadership element of your role becomes far more evident in times of crisis or change, when people will expect you to take a clear lead.

Leadership, therefore is not a role and function confined to the strategic leader or leaders at the top of the organisation. You are both managing and leading teams. Leadership qualities and characteristics are important to your ability to manage effectively.

John Adair, a well-known British thinker and writer on management, recognises the leadership component operating at all levels of management in his analysis of leadership existing at three different levels[1]:

1. **Team leadership:** of teams of about 5-20 people.
It is this area of leadership which is the main focus of this book.

2. **Operational leadership:** where you are leading and managing a number of teams whose leaders/managers report to you.

3. **Strategic leadership:** At top levels of companies, where you have overall accountability for the levels of leadership below you.

What is the manager's role?

Adair's pragmatic and simple model[2] provides a framework for thinking about the major role of management and leadership.

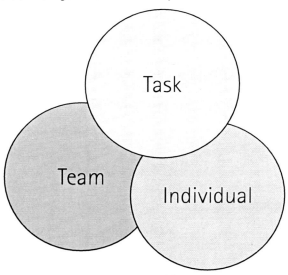

Figure 1: Management & Leadership model by Adair[2]

It is the manager's role to balance the needs of the tasks, the needs of the team or group and the needs of individuals within the team or group. These needs overlap and interrelate:

"The minutiae takes over terribly easily as a manager. Your responsibility is never to lose sight of the big picture."

What are task needs? Quite simply, what you and your team or work group are there to do. These are the team's common objectives, targets or goals.

Team or group needs consist of the processes that need attention if the team is to function cohesively and perform their tasks effectively. These include communication between the team, morale and motivation and issues around how the team is built and managed. These are considered in detail in Chapter Five.

Individual needs concern the professional development, progression and performance of people within the group and involves an understanding of how to work with a person to bring out the best in them. You can find ideas on this in Chapters Three and Four.

How do these needs interrelate?

If your team is not working together effectively, or the expectations of the task have not been communicated and understood, the tasks in hand may not get done or they may get done badly.

If individuals within the team are dissatisfied, not pulling their weight, have no sense of their role and value within the team, or do not understand what they are doing, the whole team performance may be affected, which in turn will impact on everyone's ability to achieve the tasks required.

Can a 'perfect balance' be achieved?

No. Why? Because we are working in a constantly shifting, changing environment where all the different needs are rising and falling in terms of importance and urgency.

Your role as the manager of all of this is in part concerned with an awareness that there can be detrimental consequences in allowing any set of needs to assume overriding importance for too long.

What happens when the picture looks like this for any sustained period?

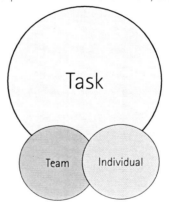

This is a picture of a task driven team, where the needs of individuals and the team are sacrificed to the needs of the tasks. Of course there will be times when this has to happen, for example when there are new deadlines, unexpected changes in legislation. For short periods, this state of affairs can be beneficial to teams and individuals, uniting people in a common goal. Hold this imbalance for too long though, and the result will be individual and team dissatisfaction. The loss of morale can start to come into play. People can only operate as workhorses for so long.

"There is a huge tension between project goals and meeting deadlines and the people management bit and it's the latter that suffers."

"In a CRO, you have got the client and the project manager on your back all the time, as a manager, you have to find a way of managing these demands and creating an environment in which people enjoy coming to work."

This scenario is also problematic if allowed to continue:

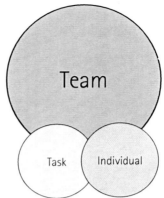

The team has become so concerned with team processes and relationships within it that this has become more important than what the team is there to do. Again there will be times when it is productive to review team processes, for example, when there is conflict in the team that needs to be addressed and resolved. You can find ideas on this in Chapters Four and Five.

"In a multinational sponsor company, the local affiliate often ends up competing with my CRO. If we win the contract, we are then faced with having to work with the affiliate organisation in the locality. They are often angry at not having got the work themselves and teamworking and communication really suffer as a result."

This scenario can also present problems when it becomes chronic:

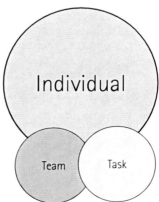

The needs of one individual have been allowed to dominate to the point where the team cannot function properly and so the tasks suffer. This is every manager's nightmare. Managing difficult behaviour is looked at in Chapter Four.

"So much of my time is taken up with one CRA whose sites always under-recruit. It's always every one else's fault and she gets upset very easily. The others have started to resent her and tell me that I spend too much time trying to support her."

What do managers do? The key tasks of a manager

If the overall role of the manager is to keep the 'big picture' in mind, to pay attention to tasks needs, team and individual needs, and how they interrelate with one another, what does a manager need to do in order to achieve this?

A survey of over 700 managers in a variety of organisations and at all levels of management, conducted at the Singapore Institute of Management identified five 'mega-components' of management[3]:

- Goal setting and review
- Creating a conducive working environment
- Managing quality
- Relating to and managing the external environment
- Managing performance

John Adair describes the functions of team leadership or management[4] as:

- Defining the talks
- Planning
- Briefing
- Controlling
- Evaluating
- Motivating
- Organising
- Providing an example

At team leadership 'people management' level, your essential tasks are:

- Setting objectives
- Building and maintaining the team
- Developing individuals
- Taking decisions
- Monitoring performance
- Resolving problems

Managers working in complex global industries are additionally expected to:

- Manage on an international scale (at team leadership level, this can mean managing remote teams, virtual teams, and teams comprising cultural diversity)
- Respond to multiple sources of authority
- Combine a variety of leadership and team roles
- Act strategically
- Utilise technology
- Communicate internally
- Communicate externally
- Establish, reinforce and develop values
- Act responsibly
- Distil complex flows of information
- Manage across functions
- Manage their own careers and personal and professional development

This is quite an exhausting list of functions, tasks and expectations, particularly when many of you also have your own workloads and targets which are not related to the managerial function.

What are the skills of an effective manager?
To create an exhaustive list of these skills at this point will be of little practical help.

The people management and interpersonal skills needed to manage effectively are considered in Chapters Three and Four.

The skills associated with defining the task, planning organising and making decisions are looked at in the next chapter.

A word on 'Emotional Intelligence '
Daniel Goleman (in his article 'What makes a leader'[5]) distilled his own theories on emotional intelligence. His basic premise is that the factors, that correlate most with success and effectiveness in life (and in leadership) are less to do with high IQ and more to do with Emotional Intelligence (EQ).

The five components of EQ are:

1. **Self-awareness:** Selfconfidence, realistic self-assessment, an informed awareness of one's strength and limitations

2. **Self-regulation:** The capacity for trustworthiness, integrity and ability to deal effectively with ambiguity and uncertainty

3. **Motivation:** Drive for achievement and openness to change, ability to recruit and retain talent

4. **Empathy:** Ability to create and maintain effective working relationships, to demonstrate understanding from another's perspective. Awareness of crosscultural factors

5. **Social skills:** skills in influencing, in persuasion, ability to build and lead teams

While some of these factors can be 'taught' and further developed, others are very much concerned with individual values and mindset.

Adair identifies the seven qualities of leadership as follows:

Enthusiasm

Integrity

Toughness

Fairness

Warmth

Humility

Confidence

If you really want to know how far you demonstrate these qualities, why not ask your staff, your peers and your boss? Remember that you are only likely to get an honest response if people trust you to listen and use the information constructively.

Chapter Two - How Do You Manage?

"We are CEOs of our own companies: Me Inc. To be in business today, our most important job is to be head marketer for the brand called You[6]

Tom Peters, *The Brand Called You, 1997*

Who is the most important manager in your life?

Is it he or she who shouts the loudest? Your most difficult member of staff?

The real answer to this question is ...you. Often the reality is very different.

"I am a clinical trials team leader and am under constant pressure to commit to timelines that are unfeasible simply because my bosses always agree to client demands without thinking through the consequences."

"One particular member of staff is always negative about any requests I make, she can get very aggressive and it's very time-consuming to deal with. I often find myself doing work which is her responsibility simply because I cannot face the effort required in dealing with her."

Self-organisation: the key to effective management
Effective management is management which gets results. It is possible to be efficient yet not effective. You can work as hard as possible to get things done. The question is, are you getting the right things done? Effective managers know how to prioritise, how to choose the right goals. They are proactive as opposed to reactive. In other words, they control the work rather than let the work control them.

What does proactive, effective working involve?
"Lord, there's never enough time for everything, help me to do a little less a little better." **Anon**

Let's look at some of the principles of self-organisation, using a series of statements about managing time and prioritising. Before you read the commentary under each statement, stop to think about how far you agree or disagree with it.

1. Most people know exactly what their time management problems are.

   If this were true, we would be working in a far more effective world. It is often the case that people will blame anything and anybody rather than look at their own strengths and limitations in this area. How many times have you heard people in the office consistently blame external events and the demands of others for poor time management? How many people do you know who are unable to make decisions? Are disorganised? Unable to prioritise? How many of those people recognise that they have at least some part to play in this state of affairs? For many of them, the problems exist 'out there'.

Effective self-management starts with recognising that we need to take some responsibility for the way in which we manage work. We need to recognise how far we contribute to inefficient and ineffective work practices.

"I'm not very organised, I prefer to act on impulse and can get carried away with new ideas on the spur of the moment. I can see that some of my staff find it difficult to work like this and I need to learn to be a little more methodical in my approach. People get very irritated if they can't locate me when they need me, and they often can't because I forget to keep my diary up to date."

2. People who use time wisely usually find time for really important work activities.

   Wise people know what NOT to do. They can prioritise effectively.

   ### The 80/20 rule
   Italian Economist Vilfredo Pareto created a mathematical principle known as Pareto's principle in 1906, which states that twenty per cent of work activities produce eighty per cent of results. Effective management is about identifying and recognising that twenty per cent. Most of the important results you achieve stem from only a handful of work activities. Busy does not equal effective and hard work is no substitute for proactive self-organisation.

   "People find it difficult to say 'no' in CR and they end up having more and more work piled on them – learning to say no has been the most important step towards being able to think proactively about my workload."

   ### Parkinson's Law
   The British Academic Northcote Parkinson observed that work expands to fill the time available for its completion. In other words, if people have three months to complete a task, it will take them at least that long, even if they had the time and space to complete it in one month.

3. Time spent trying to achieve perfection is always time well spent.

   At first sight, this might seem to be a true statement. For perfectionists, it can be a way of life. However, in the messy business of people management and in a rapidly changing work climate, what can perfect really mean? Is there any such thing as the 'perfect' solution? How can we know that your idea of perfect is the same as mine?

   In many of the things that we do, if we can deliver eighty per cent of perfection, we are doing an effective job. The next time you find yourself striving for perfection, ask yourself: what am I really trying to satisfy here? The needs of the task or my need to be perfect?

The Institute of Clinical Research

4. In most jobs, people use their time in repetitive patterns that can be analysed.

    Where your job is varied and diverse, it is easy to think that the above statement must be false since no two days are the same. In reality, we are creatures of habit and form patterns of working. Think about the way you like to manage your day: what do you like to do first thing? When are you most likely to read mail? Emails? Have a break? Make phone calls? Even if you spend a considerable amount of time travelling, your days in the office will have some preferred structure to them. You will also have developed some consistent work habits while travelling.

    "If I was honest, it's become a habit with me to be constantly available, I feel bad if I don't pick up the phone as soon as it rings, or answer emails immediately. It's as if dealing with constant interruptions has become a habit. You spend all day answering the phone and at the end of it, the protocol you are supposed to be reviewing is still sitting there."

    To gain a better understanding of how you work, it is worth spending some time thinking about the patterns that you have developed. Ask yourself: how effective are they? Have I slipped into habitual ways of working that are ineffective and can be improved? When am I most likely to waste time? What tasks or situations cause me to procrastinate? At what part of the day am I at my best and when do I work least well? How effective am I at scheduling difficult tasks at times when I am likely to be working optimally?

5. It is always better to wait until you have collected the relevant information before making a decision.

    In a working world which requires the ability to make speedy decisions, you cannot always wait until you have all the information that you would like. There will be times when just what constitutes relevant information will be unclear and you have to go ahead and make a decision based on the data available. As individuals, we will experience these situations with differing degrees of comfort. For some new managers, making decisions without the relevant information can be very frightening. Whether we are new or more experienced in management, some of us are more comfortable with making decisions based on incomplete information than others.

    "At first I used to feel terrified at having to make decisions without all the information I felt I needed. I've learned that I often just need to do this. Particularly around allocation of resources based on incomplete work projections. If you don't know what the study will finally involve its hard to know how many CRAs to allocate, but then if I don't make some kind of decision, I risk losing out and so do my staff."

Effective decision making skills: positive uncertainty

If working effectively is about choosing the right goals, it is also about knowing when to adapt, modify or let those goals go altogether. It's about knowing when to recognise that what was right yesterday is not right today, being focused and flexible about what we want.

People usually argue for one or the other.

Argument for focus:
If you don't know where you're going, you'll probably end up somewhere else!

Argument for flexibility:
If you always know where you're going, you may never end up somewhere else!

An effective planner and decision-maker is one who is: "Goal guided, not goal governed." In other words, focused and flexible.

This is a paradoxical state of affairs and forms the foundation of 'positive uncertainty'.

"I have learned to be very careful about the patient recruitment targets I will agree to, especially when a site has not recruited as expected and the sponsor wants to set another deadline date. As far as I can, I'll build in as much leeway as possible because I can never be one hundred per cent certain. And basically to make as sure as possible that we can actually deliver. What's the point of caving into targets that you know from the outset are unrealistic?"

6. Frequent interruptions to plans make setting priorities unproductive

    You will achieve very little satisfaction in work if you don't keep end goals or objectives in mind. You will simply be reacting. The challenge here is to be flexible enough to change and modify priorities where necessary. Yes, situations change and yes, we need to adapt and modify our priorities accordingly. If you lose sight of what you are trying to achieve, how will you know whether you are wasting time?

    "It's so easy to get sucked into day-to-day underperformance that you can completely lose sight of what you are supposed to be aiming for. I need to step back and make sure that I still know where I'm going, even if the goals are now different. If I lose sight of it all, my team is definitely going to suffer."

7. How you manage your time directly influences you effectiveness in supervising and monitoring your team.

    "It's not enough to be busy. The question is: 'What are you busy about'?"

    Henry Thoreau

    The manager who works all hours, does not take holidays and is poor at maintaining an effective work-life balance is sending mixed messages to her staff. You may encourage your staff to manage their time constructively but people learn by example. They will not do what you say but what you do.

"There is a great pressure on managers in CR to get in earlier and leave later than anyone else. This expectation is really unhelpful to setting an example for work-life balance and it means that many good people leave when they start to want a better quality of life. Trying to juggle work, home and children and being expected to do long hours and travel eventually causes burn-out."

Equally, the manager who is disorganised, unable to make decisions and prioritise does not provide a good role model for their staff.

8. In the short term, delegation to staff will always result in time savings for you.

This is blatantly false since it takes time to delegate effectively. This often means that we save time by doing it all ourselves. In the long run this is counter productive as we lose time by failing to share workload appropriately. Staff lose out on the opportunity to take on new challenges and progress professionally. For information on effective delegation and on levels of delegation, see 'the manager as delegator', later on in this chapter.

Poor self-management: what to avoid

Adair identifies five stereotypical behaviours of a poor self-manager[7]:

- A poor delegator
- A bad organiser
- An excellent procrastinator
- A poor performer at meetings
- A purposeless executive

Self-management starts with an honest and critical review of how you manage time and tasks. You could complete a SWOT analysis (strengths, weaknesses, opportunities, threats) on your organisational capabilities. Be as specific as you can possibly be about any of these factors since the more specific we are about something, the more likely we are to be able to utilise it or manage it.

Strengths in self-organisation	Weaknesses in self-organisation
Opportunities (What conditions or circumstances will help me improve my self-organisation?)	Threats (What conditions or circumstances stop me becoming more organised?)

Making meetings work

How often have you heard people say that they have to attend so many meetings that they do not have time to get on with work? Conversely, it would seem that the only thing worse then being invited to too many meetings, is not being invited.

The fear of being left out or missing something important means that people will attend whether or not the meeting is useful or relevant to them. Meetings can become a substitute for actually getting on with work.

Your challenge is twofold. First, ask yourself how many of the meetings that you attend are useful and relevant to you? Where the answer is negative, is there any way in which you can influence the meeting so they do fulfil your needs? Would it be appropriate for someone else to go in your place? What would you stand to lose or gain by choosing not to go?

Your second challenge concerns making the meetings that you are responsible for purposeful and productive.

Successful meetings management: five key questions

When it comes to planning meetings Adair suggest that you ask yourself the following five questions:

- Why are we meeting?

- What would be the result of not having the meeting, or what should result from having it?

- Who should attend?

- How long should it be and how should it be structured?

- When is the best time to hold it?

The hallmarks of successful meetings

Meetings are planned ahead. The agenda and supporting papers are circulated well in advance.

The agenda is specific. People know what they will be meeting to discuss as opposed to some vague heading.

The agenda has been thought through so that the most important items come first, it is realistic and there is a good possibility that it can be covered in the time available at the meeting.

There is clarity of outcomes from the meeting. That is, things get decided.

Minutes are concise and action oriented with responsibilities allocated.

You, as the chair, or convenor of the meeting act as an effective steer through the agenda, encouraging people to take part in the discussion, moving them back on track when they digress, and ensuring that there is clarity of decision, outcomes and responsibilities.

You and your management style

One of the frequently asked questions from people new to management is: 'how do I know that I am using the right style of management?'

There is a simple answer to this: there is no right style of management. Your style of management will be different to other people's styles, simply because you are you. While you can learn from the example of others, learn from reading and attending courses and learn from experience, you will interpret that learning in a way that makes sense for you. And you never stop learning. Developing your management style is a process which takes place over time. The best managers are those who are always prepared to critically reappraise their approaches, whatever their level and stage of experience.

"Over the last ten years, I've become a lot less impatient with my teams and with myself. I used to want everything done by yesterday. I'm learning that to get the best out of some people you sometimes need to be less driven with them, not everyone wants to work so hectically."

The key to effective and flexible management is the ability to access a variety of styles, appropriate to the needs of individuals and the needs of the tasks.

Situational Leadership before Ken Blanchard

Ken Blanchard offers one useful and accessible framework for this in his model for 'Situational Leadership'[8]. The following is a condensed summary of the theory and is designed to do no more than introduce you to it.

Situational leadership identifies four styles of management/leadership:

The leader/manager as:

Style 1. Director

Style 2. Coach

Style 3. Facilitator or supporter

Style 4. Delegator

A style one leader is an example of autocratic leadership or management. Style four leadership can be seen as an example of democratic leadership or management

What do the four styles involve?
In the directing style, the manager will set the standards, give the orders or instructions and very closely supervise and monitor work performance.

In coaching style, the manager is in the role of expert guide. While she continues to closely supervise and monitor performance, she will also work collaboratively with staff, eliciting suggestions, explaining decisions, and involving them in problem solving.

In facilitation or supporting style, the manager provides the resources and any help or advice sought by staff and shares decision-making responsibility with them.

In delegating style, the leader or manager passes over responsibility for the work or project to others on the grounds that they have the expertise and experience to accomplish the tasks. The manager continues to remain accountable. Delegation to others does not mean blaming them if things go wrong. It does mean taking responsibility for your decision to delegate that particular work activity.

How will I know which styles to use?
Blanchard uses an old saying to support his theory:

"Different strokes for different folks."

The key to managing effectively is to know which style to use in which situation with which person.

Consider the following examples:

Katrina is brand new to the role of CRA. She is keen to learn but lacks any experience in your company or in any others.

What style is most appropriate here?

Style one: Katrina needs to know and understand the importance of the very basics. It is vital that you give clear direction, set standards and expectations, issue clear instructions and closely supervise work performance. Otherwise, you are setting her up to fail.

Adam is the administrator for your team. He is experienced in the role and has been working well until the last few months, when he has become bored with the role and the standard of his work has fallen.

You might consider style two leadership. Adam knows his job but is in need of motivation, he needs to be re-energised with the potential and possibilities of the role. As coach, you can work with him to raise standards and set new goals for professional development.

Johan is very competent but lacks confidence and will tend to say no to new responsibilities.

Style three could work here with a little of style two where necessary. With support, Johan can develop confidence and recognise his strengths as well as his limitations.

Katharine has just joined your team from elsewhere in the organisation. She comes with a reputation for being excellent at budgeting and forecasting. This is not your strong point and you know that you will need to submit your resource allocations for the next financial year in the next six weeks.

Style four makes sense here. Katharine is experienced and competent. You could afford to take an informed risk on delegating this piece of work to her.

However, Katharine has joined your team because she will have the opportunity to project manage a phase IV trial. This will be the first time she has been in this role and she is anxious to do well. She has several years experience working as a part of a project team.

A mixture of style two and three could be appropriate here. This means that you are using style four to manage Katharine in one area of her work and style two in others.

Isn't using different styles for different people unfair?
Not if you agree on the best ways to work with them in dialogue with them.

Blanchard asserts that situational leadership is not something you do to people, but something you do with them. He calls this process 'contracting' and it starts with setting goals or objectives with staff and then deciding with them how best to work together to achieve these.

Beware 'getting stuck' in styles

Situational leadership theory suggests that we may have one or two preferred management styles and these we tend to overuse if not mindful. Most of us can think of a manager who conforms solely to style one leadership. They are only comfortable when issuing orders and controlling the work of others. We can probably all think of managers who confuse effective management with constantly being in supportive mode. They are very uncomfortable with being directive and operate from the position that 'good' management must always be supportive and nurturing. Equally, some managers are really so good at delegation that they are left with little to do!

Under pressure, it is suggested that we may revert to one end of the scale or the other. Some of us become very style one and desperately attempt to control and contain. Others take flight to the extreme end of style four and became unable to do anything at all, hoping that someone else will sort it all out.

How do I know which are my preferred styles?

According to situational leadership, your goal as a manager is to learn to use all four styles flexibly and judiciously. Develop the styles that you feel least comfortable with. Learn to use less of the styles you feel most comfortable with. Recognise that different people need to be treated in different ways if you want to get the best from them.

How to develop your management style:

- Observe those that you admire: what is it about their style that works? (Be wary about simply trying to emulate others, you need to adopt and adapt from the examples of others and integrate them into your own styles and approaches.)

- Adopt an open mindset

- Be prepared to make and learn from mistakes

- Get supervision yourself

- Find a mentor

- Read and attend courses

- Ask questions of yourself and others

- Ask your team to give you specific and constructive feedback about their experience of you as a manager

- Be prepared to learn from experience by reflecting on your performance

Reflection is the capacity to think about the things we have experienced in a systematic or organised way, evaluate those experiences and then learn from them.

What is reflective practice?
Reflective practice is where you as a manager, take a step back from the work you are doing in order to review and analyse how well the work is progressing and how effectively you are working. The following descriptions of reflective practice are taken from the work of Donald Schon[9], the foremost writer on the subject.

When does it take place?
You can do it on the job. This is known as 'reflection-in-action'. In other words you are reviewing as you are working, weighing up and assessing a course of action as you take it.

You might also choose to reflect after the event and this is known as 'reflection-on-action'.

We are, ideally, aiming to reflect or think about what is going on during and after the event. This is described as 'reflection-in-and-on-action'.

Why is it important?
Most of us will reflect on our work to some degree already. We do it on an occasional basis, when we have time, or when something goes drastically wrong and we have to review. A commitment to ongoing and organised reflection is vital if we want to improve and learn as managers. If we are simply too busy doing the job to take the time to think about what we are doing, the quality of work will suffer.

How can you improve as a reflective practitioner?
Ask the right questions!

Reflection usually involves asking a series of questions about your work and the ways in which you are approaching it.

To take an example: you may have just had a meeting with your team.

As a reflective practitioner, you might then ask yourself some or all of the following questions:

- How far did I achieve what I wanted to achieve?
- Was there anything I could have/should have done differently?
- What can I learn from the event?
- What might I do differently next time?

Processing, thinking about and answering questions like this can help you gain insight into your work and the way you work. It can help you learn about and improve your practice.

The manager as delegator

Knowing how to delegate, when to delegate and who to delegate to, is an essential managerial art. Delegation makes sense when there are many jobs to be done, when someone has the expertise and/or the time to do the job better than you can or when delegation represents a developmental opportunity for someone.

Outlined below are six levels of delegation. As you read them, think about the levels that you feel most comfortable with.

Six levels of delegation

1. Carry out the work under my constant supervision:

    This is most commonly used with new members of staff. The manager is in constant contact with the task, they control how the work should be done and carry all the decision-making responsibility for it.

2. Carry out the work in this way and consult me before taking any action:

    Both the process and the outcome are specified by the manager. The staff member will plan the work but must consult before committing themselves or the organisation to any risky decisions.

3. Carry out the work as you see fit but report back to me before taking any action:

    The process is left to the staff member's discretion but the manager retains final control before the final decisions are taken.

4. Carry out the work and report back regularly on what you've done:

    The process is left to the staff member's discretion and they have freedom to act but must report after the fact. This level will tend to be used only with people in whom you have a reasonable level of confidence.

5. Carry out the work and report back only when you encounter difficulties:

    This is the level of delegation we have with our senior staff. It is assumed that their decision making and performance levels are problem free unless they tell us otherwise.

6. This is your project – achieve the objectives in whatever way you see fit:

    This is the highest level of delegation and in reality used very rarely. At this level, the staff member has complete discretion and carries complete responsibility, although not accountability for the task. You have that.

How do these levels of delegation relate to the four leadership styles?

Managers who like to control or who are perfectionists tend to find it difficult to delegate above levels one and two. Essentially, they remain in the 'director' role when delegating. A manager whose basic approach to management is a style one approach, regardless of the expertise or experience of their staff, will tend to see delegation in terms of levels one or two. Conversely, managers who are keen to enable staff can sometimes delegate at a stage inappropriately high for an individual's level of expertise, experience and competence. They then risk setting people up to fail or to become demoralised. In other words, leaders and managers whose basic approach to management is style three or four, might delegate at levels five or six before their staff are ready and able to deal with this level of delegated responsibility.

"In my early career as a manager, I was so keen to empower and support people that I gave one individual too much responsibility too early and there were real problems. She had neither the experience nor the skills to run the project without a good deal of help from me. I can now see that I needed to be much more directive in the way in which I delegated until she had a better understanding of the expectations and requirements of the job."

Chapter Three - Managing Performance

What are the basic principles?

The following checklist is a useful guide to the foundations of effective performance management. You will need:

- Clear procedures for recruiting staff. You need to be clear about the expectations and requirements of the job and the knowledge skills and attitudes you need from the post holder before you recruit. If you are not specific about what you want from either the post or the person in the first place, then it is difficult to manage performance effectively

- Planned induction for all staff. The more comprehensive the induction period, the more likely it is that you will empower new staff to perform to the best of their abilities. People need to know the expectations of the job. Time and effort is required to enable them to meet these and to settle into the team, department and organisation. For more information on this, see stages in staff development on page 29 and team cycles on page 52.

- Clear and transparent procedures for deciding what needs doing, deadlines and standards

- Clear and transparent procedures for monitoring work to be sure that it is being done adequately

- Training and support to help workers do their jobs, or do them better

Once the new staff member is sufficiently familiar with their responsibilities and targets have been agreed, line management sessions then allow for regular monitoring on a day-to-day, week-to-week and month-to-month basis.

Appraisal enables the staff member and their manager to take an overview of performance, to look back on the year and to create a forward plan. Appraisal can be seen as a line management session, which occurs annually and which provides an opportunity to review overall performance and to plan ahead.

How to get the best out of line management

- The line manager must have adequate information about the staff member's role. Two of the most common complaints from workers about management are that managers either demonstrate little understanding of what a staff member actually does or that they fail to demonstrate that they can view the demands of the job from the staff member's perspective

- There are clear standards against which to monitor or evaluate work and performance. What gets measured gets managed. If objectives are unclear, how can you ascertain whether they are being met? See page 28 for information on objective setting

- There are agreed procedures for arranging and carrying out sessions, for recording issues, topics and actions agreed

- There is a clear policy about confidentiality. Trust is vital to a relationship which is to be transparent and honest. Staff must feel that information on their performance will not be inappropriately shared

- There should be a commitment to making time for formal line management sessions. See page 32 for types of line management

A clear distinction is made between line management and disciplinary procedures

Disciplinary procedures start only when line management, including appraisal, has failed. It is vital that you are aware of your organisation's policies on disciplinary and grievance procedures.

Key factors for successful line management sessions:

- Preparation (by both manager and staff member)

- A constructive focus, on what can be improved as opposed to what is going wrong

- A clear boundary between work-related and personal support

- The ability to remain patient and calm, ask questions and listen

- The ability to come to an agreed set of specific actions to address work related issues, problems or concerns

- The ability to translate these into action plans, with timelines

"'My most positive line management experiences are where I have been given enough time with my line manager, where I feel that they know what I have been doing and where I do not feel I am left to fly solo. Someone who takes the time to say thank you and acknowledges what I have done."

How to structure a line management session

The following is one format for individual line management sessions. It should be modified to suit different settings.

Preparing for the session

- Set the sessions in advance, so that they are a regular feature in the diary

- Try to avoid sessions first thing on a Monday morning or last thing on a Friday afternoon

- Review the record of the previous session and note items and action plans that need following up. This should form the basis for an agreed agenda

Making the most of the session

- Start the session on time. If you don't make it a priority, neither will your staff member

The Institute of Clinical Research

- Clarify the agenda and add any additional business

- Within the first ten minutes, always 'take the temperature' by asking general questions

- However important the agenda, it always makes sense to find out just where your staff member is starting from. Also check whether there are likely to be any avoidable interruptions (these should be really exceptional). Prioritise the agenda together

- Review the work on the agenda. Agree and record action plans

- Review other work or projects

- Look at the developmental, training or personal issues related to work

- Share any information/briefing

- Make notes on the session that you both agree on

Making the most of appraisal

What is an appraisal?

Appraisal is a process which is used to take stock of an individual's performance and provides an excellent opportunity to formally recognise achievements.

An appraisal usually covers a known review period and is often an annual event. It has at its heart a face-to-face discussion and results in a clear action plan for performance maintenance or improvement.

An appraisal reviews progress and achievement and also looks forward to what happens next. It explores the continuing professional development needs of the individual. For example, through clarifying objectives, coaching, monitoring, training and development goals.

In a great many ways, appraisal can be seen as a line management session 'writ large'. The central differences being that appraisals are usually longer since they cover a greater time period, they are also potentially more 'formal' since copies of appraisals are lodged on file and may be seen by other members of the organisation.

There should be no surprises in appraisals. Effective ongoing line management can result in both you and your staff member having a very clear idea of strengths, problems and areas for development before the event.

You and your staff need to know and understand the format and expectations of your organisation's appraisal system and work within the system in the way which makes the best sense for the needs of the job and the staff member.

Here is a checklist of pitfalls to avoid when preparing for and running an appraisal session with one of your staff.

Appraisal: how not to do it!

- Make it obvious that spotting serious weaknesses and laying blame is a major goal of the process

- Do not focus on achievements but on faults

- Take copious notes, which the staff member cannot see

- Alternatively, don't take any notes, so that any reports you have to write are comprised of sketchy and hazy memory

- Fit three or four appraisals into one hour with a watch placed on your desk

- Surprise your staff member by saving up all your criticisms of their work for the review process

- Do not make any preparation for a review and do not encourage your staff to prepare either

- Constantly cancel reviews, as you have far more important things to do

- Always answer the phone in the middle of a review

- Undermine the process, by telling your staff that you think it's a waste of time anyway

- Make sure your staff know that appraisal is a one way process, you judging them.

- Make sure that you do all the talking

- Ask very few questions (and answer them yourself)

And how to make it work...

The skills required to make the appraisal process work are the skills involved in effective people leadership and management on a day-to day basis. Many, if not all of the skills and attitudes addressed in this book, are involved in effective appraisal.

They include skills in communication, particularly listening, negotiation, emotional intelligence, clarity and articulation. These are combined with abilities to organise time and tasks, set clear and agreed goals and objectives and attend to continuing professional development needs.

Managing Performance and Setting Objectives

What are the benefits of setting objectives?

Defining clear targets or objectives for individual staff members makes good sense on a number of levels:

- It helps to ensure that they are clear about what they are trying to accomplish and how their work fits into the work of your team and the organisation as a whole

The Institute of Clinical Research

- People have something concrete to work towards. Their progress can be measured (remember, what gets measured, gets managed) and they will gain a sense of accomplishment

How to set objectives
One model for doing this is the **SMARTER** approach.

Targets, goals or objectives should be:

Specific
What exactly is the objective? The more specific it is, the more measurable it is. An objective such as 'work on study newsletter' is really too broad. Reframing this as 'design and distribute study newsletter to internal and external team by x date' gives far greater clarification on expectations of performance.

Measurable
As far as you can, create goals with tangibly measurable outcomes. 'Improve speed of data query repsonse' is less easily measured than ' reduce data query response time from one working week to four days.'

Agreed
The more your staff member 'owns' the goal, sees it as relevant to their work and actively buys into what is to be achieved and how to achieve it, the more likely it is that the objective will be reached.

Realistic
All things considered, for example, time and other work commitments, how realistically achievable is this goal?

Time-related
What are the timelines for this? Setting realistic milestones and deadlines for objectives helps people to organise their work to meet the goal. Open-ended timelines usually mean that tasks are put off.

Evaluated and Reviewed
There is little point in setting objectives and then never referring to them again (a common mistake in appraisal). For objectives or goals to remain alive, relevant and current they need to be regularly reviewed, monitored and adapted as necessary. The responsibility for this is held jointly by yourself and your staff member.

When does it make sense to set objectives?
The appraisal session provides an ideal opportunity for setting objectives or goals for the next year. Within this framework, line management then offers an opportunity for monitoring the individual's performance against those targets, identifying problems or obstacles encountered in meeting the targets and any

changes (internal or external) or personal circumstances that may affect the individual's performance.

The induction of new staff is also an important time for setting objectives. They provide a clear framework for progression and for measuring progress.

Objective setting could in fact occur at any point in a working year. The advent of new projects, a restructure, new technology, the need for new challenges and opportunities, all create potential for focused yet flexible goals.

Stages of staff development
All of us go through the following stages in any job role. Effective line management is essential to ensuring optimum performance at any stage.

The following figure shows the stages of development that people go through in any job. Running through all these stages is line management, as indicated by the arrow on the right of the figure.

Induction
Settling into the organisation. Learning to do the job
The line manager's tasks: to set the standards and expectations, clarify lines of support and accountability

Inclusion
Becoming part of the team and organisation
Sharing the same values, aims and objectives
The line manager's tasks: to get to know staff and how best to work with them, to support and encourage involvement.

Competence
Becoming able to carry out all aspects of the job effectively
The line manager's tasks: to coach and support performance

Further development
Developing the job to provide new challenges
The line manager's tasks: working with staff in career planning, identifying new opportunities and challenges

Plateau
Limit of development opportunities reached
The line manager's tasks: work with staff to consider options for the future

Transition
Change to a new role/job to develop skills
The line manager's tasks: constructive support

LINE MANAGEMENT

The Institute of Clinical Research

Types of line management/performance management

The table below sets out four different types of line management together with how and when they are used

Formal and unplanned	Formal and planned
These happen at times of unforeseen crisis or urgency. It may be vital that some space and time is created away from the situation to work on the problem.	Line management takes the form of planned meetings. There is an agreed agenda and an agreed way of working. Such meetings can be arranged for a limited or indefinite period of time, for general or specific purposes. The outcomes of these sessions are usually recorded in writing.
Informal and unplanned	**Informal and planned**
Again, this might happen in the event of unforeseen circumstances. Line management is given through constructive feedback, demonstration or example. This may become the focus for discussion in a more formal context.	Agreements are reached between the line manager and staff to provide ad hoc advice, support and constructive feedback during the course of work. How this is provided may also be the subject of agreement.

Chapter Four - Managing people

The manager as communicator

How does communication work?

Two models of communication are useful to explore when thinking about how to communicate effectively with your staff.

1. The Transmittal Model

This is oneway communication, for example, radio or television.

In times of crisis or urgency, many managers use this type of communication to tell people what to do. Some managers work in transmittal mode all of the time. They simply assume that what they have said has been understood fully and completely in exactly the way that they intended it to be understood. Most, if not all of us, use this approach to communication in certain circumstances and we are often surprised to discover that what we thought we were communicating has been understood very differently. Email is the vehicle for communication most frequently misunderstood in the workplace. This too, operates 'transmittally'. In other words, there is no room for clarifying understanding in one-way communication.

In fact, all communication, *even if it is delivered transmittally*, operates according to our second model of communication.

2. The Transformational Model

Meaning is derived from the way in which communication is understood and interpreted by the receiver. Any group of us could watch the same television programme, but in discussion, we would discover that we all had differing interpretations and reactions to the content.

We interpret communication differently according to the 'frames of reference' each one of us brings to any interaction. These are the 'lenses' or 'windows' through which we view the world. All of us have a unique set of these lenses. They are made up of myriad factors, which make us the people that we are. Background, culture, race, sexuality, education, past experience, beliefs, upbringing, gender are just some of these. Our lenses are not fixed but are constantly changing.

The Institute of Clinical Research

More prosaically, how we are feeling on any particular day, whether or not we had a good journey to work, our general mood, will also influence the way in which we interpret communication. What is said to us after a hard and frustrating day may well be heard differently if it is said to us when we are rested the next morning.

Our perceptions of the communicator will also influence our understanding. If a manager that we respect and trust praises our work, we are more likely to hear that praise as genuine than if a manager we distrust praises our work. They may say exactly the same thing but we will interpret or understand it differently.

Given the sheer complexity of interaction, the uniqueness of the individual frames of reference though which we view things, what is surprising is not that communication fails but that it ever succeeds. Einstein once commented: "the major problem with communication is the illusion that it has occurred".

Communication: how can you avoid misunderstandings?

Effective communicators do not assume that they have been heard and understood or that they hear and understand. They take time to ask questions, to seek clarification, to summarise, to test out and check out understanding. This is particularly important when working with people from different nationalities and cultures. They recognise that effective communication is always a two way process, that no two people will understand things in quite the same way, that different people need different communication approaches, that it takes time to thoroughly establish that people have understood.

Effective communication involves being very clear yourself concerning the message you are trying to convey. If you are not clear about what you are trying to say, then there is very little chance that anyone else will be. This often means thorough preparation and careful attention to the danger of making assumptions about what people do or do not know.

The most effective people managers communicate in a way that demonstrates that they know their staff, their needs and expectations. They take time to discover the best ways to communicate with particular individuals in order to build the most productive and constructive working relationships. An insightful manager recognises that the way in which they personally would ideally like to be communicated with is not necessarily the best and most effective approach for each of their staff. They treat others as they need to be treated.

"I am a very task-oriented person, I respond well to direct communication which does not waste time and is to the point. I have had to recognise that some of my staff find this approach a little uncaring and insensitive. I've learned that to build good working relationships with them I've needed to take more time to listen and talk a little more about how people feel about their work. It's been hard, as I don't need this for myself."

If you can build bridges and create constructive and productive channels of communication with your staff, you will find that you have the foundations that are essential for playing your part in enabling people to work to their optimum, to play to their strengths, address their areas for development and tap into their motivation for work.

How to get the best from people: understanding motivation
What motivates people in the workplace?

Let's start with you and what motivates you. Why do you do the job that you do?

The answer to this question is complex. Yes, you may well need enough money to live and to provide for a family. You may also enjoy the challenge, you may need the structure and security work gives you. You may be ambitious or see work as providing you with status and self-respect. For some of us work is closely bound up with identity and self-worth. If things are not going well at work, then this dramatically affects self-esteem. For others, work is more of a way to fund life outside work although this does not mean that we do not want to do a good job.

It's worth taking a few minutes to consider seriously why it is that you work. What do you get out of it? What do you value about work? What motivates and drives you in the workplace? Below are some factors, which can be considered as motivating factors, or reasons why we work. Choose the five that you think most closely reflect the things you most value. If your values are not reflected on this list, then add to it.

Belonging	Fast pace	Security
Helping others	Friendship	Problem solving
Independence	Change and variety	Work with others
Recognition	Status	Customer contact
Achievement	Adventure	Work alone
High earnings	Stability	Health
Excitement	Competition	Balance
Physical challenge	Pressure	Precision work
Time freedom	Flexibility	Power and authority
Order	Quality	Integrity
Personal development	Loyalty	Creative expression

Your answers will be unique to you. The answers of your staff may well be different to yours. There can sometimes be a tendency to assume that what motivates and drives us either must or should be what is motivating and driving others. This can cause all sorts of misunderstandings and miscommunications. Just because you are ambitious/insecure/demoralised/optimistic does not mean that others are or should be.

The Institute of Clinical Research

The Iceberg theory

All we can know of a person is what they choose to show us. We see their behaviour. We do not see the intentions behind the behaviour. Imagine an iceberg. All we see the tip of the iceberg. What we cannot know are the attitudes, thoughts, values and feelings below the surface which underpin that behaviour.

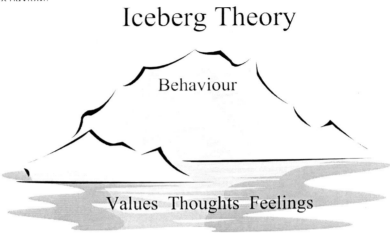

Iceberg Theory

Behaviour

Values Thoughts Feelings

We can start to make informed judgements about what underpins people's behaviour only through building a relationship with the person. A person needs to feel safe in order to be willing and able to share the motivation behind what they do.

It is remarkably easy to jump to conclusions about the reason why a person behaves as they behave. This is dangerous. An effective people manager avoids making rash judgements about the motivation of others. They seek first to understand. This is important because if you are not clear why someone is behaving in a particular way, or you have made an erroneous decision about why, you may well approach the situation inappropriately. You then risk alienating them and damaging the relationship you have.

The manager as detective

There is an old Yiddish proverb: 'Ten lands may be more easily known than one person'.

All of your staff will have their own particular motivations. Remember 'different strokes for different folks'.

Effective managers approach people with an open mind. They practise the art of asking questions as opposed to making statements about the behaviour of others and suspend judgement until they have carried out a certain amount of detective work.

The Institute of Clinical Research

"We had a man in our team who rarely spoke, who never seemed interested in getting to know people, just got on with his work and never joined in with any social activities. We all found him cold and aloof and gave up on him really. It wasn't until he left that we discovered that his wife was very sick the whole time he was working with us and he had had to leave work to take care of her."

Attitudes and assumptions : 'Theory X' and 'Theory Y'

We have seen that the way in which we approach and interpret the behaviour of the people that we manage is very much dependant on our own attitudes and mindsets about why we and others behave in certain ways.

Douglas McGregor, an industrial psychologist, considered two polarised sets of assumptions about people at work, which he labelled 'Theory X ' and 'Theory Y'. [10]

The 'Theory X' manager believes that if given the opportunity, people will work as little as possible. They need to be coerced, controlled and directed to work. On the whole people are motivated by the need for security as opposed to ambition.

The' Theory Y' manager believes that work satisfaction is an intrinsic part of a person's sense of identity. They are self-motivated to do a competent job. Given the right circumstances or conditions, they will accept responsibility and will actively seek out opportunities for progression. Where people feel committed, they will demonstrate self-direction and self-management.

McGregor found that autocratic managers who make all the decisions and hold all the power tend to assume a 'Theory X' view of people.

Democratic leaders who share the responsibility with staff and involve them in planning and decision-making assume a 'Theory Y' view of people.

His experiments with 'Theory X' and 'Theory Y' showed that both approaches can be effective. He did, however, consistently find that staff disliked managers who claimed to be 'Y' but who acted 'X' under pressure.

"I had a manager who claimed to always put his people first and when things were going well, he was friendly and approachable, but when the sponsor complained about something, he always became a dictator and would not listen to us."

As a rule, intelligent people need to agree rather than obey and a 'Theory Y' mindset is most appropriate in these circumstances.

Ask yourself the following:

How far am I a 'Theory X' or 'Theory Y' manager?

What circumstances or people bring out the 'Theory X' in me?

What circumstances or people bring out the 'Theory Y' in me?

How far do my underpinning beliefs about individuals or groups enhance or interfere with my capacity to make informed judgements about the behaviour of others?

Managing difficult behaviour

There are a few people in the world that everyone finds 'difficult'. However, it is unlikely that such people are always difficult in all areas of life. The reasons why people are difficult are wide-ranging: from poor self-esteem through to crisis situations in one area of life that spill out into another. For example, a person may be difficult at work because they are experiencing problems at home.

When faced with a 'difficult person', we may make all sorts of assumptions about why they behave as they behave. Unless that person chooses to tell us, we cannot know whether our assumptions are correct. The danger is that we tend to turn these assumptions into 'truths' about a person and these beliefs subsequently affect the way in which we interact with them.

Difficult behaviour: is it absolute or relative?

As individuals, we perceive difficult behaviour differently. A person who, for example, values emotional disclosure, may find someone who is closed and reserved difficult to deal with. Some people find supreme self-confidence admirable, others will resent it and view that person as arrogant. What we perceive as difficult people or difficult behaviour is largely relative and is dependent on our own unique frames of reference.

Strategies for dealing with difficult behaviour and difficult communication

- **Separate the behaviour from the person**

It may well be that a 'difficult person' is difficult in certain areas or over certain things. It can help to see the difficult behaviour as just that, difficult behaviour in certain circumstances. It does not mean that the person is always difficult.

"We have an excellent head of data management although he is inflexible when it comes to agreed timelines. He will not negotiate at all on changes and it can make life very difficult for us."

- **Accept that you cannot change anyone else**

The only person you can change is yourself: your responses, your attitudes and your reactions.

- **Make the most of situations that present themselves**

Learn to develop assertive behaviour, so that you are neither crushed nor angered by situations

When dealing with a difficult relationship, you cannot expect to get everything you want from a situation. Even if you do not achieve one hundred per cent of what you wanted, if you are able to achieve most of it, in as short a time as possible and with as little disruption as possible, you can be pleased with yourself.

Many people believe that if they do not hold out for everything they want, they are being either weak or submissive. This is not so. It shows a maturity and strength of character to be able to propose or accept compromise in cases where no principles are at stake.

• Adjust your own behaviour

It is always wise to ask yourself: "How far have my actions or omissions contributed to this situation?" This is not the same as blaming yourself. It may be that your approach to the situation is exacerbating it and it may be time to try a different approach.

"One of my staff members felt that another was consistently underperforming. It was a multi-cultural team and at the root of this was a cultural clash, they were just not speaking the same language. I did not see this at the time and expected them to sort their problems out on their own. With hindsight, I needed to have taken a more interventionist approach from the outset. As a manager, you are desperately short of time and overworked and in the interests of saving time, I did not spend the time needed on this problem, it was a false economy. My contribution to the problem was that I mis-prioritised my time"

• Choose your 'battles'

You need to be clear about how important and how worthwhile it is to find a way through a particularly difficult situation. Given that you cannot change others, only yourself, there may also be times when you will need to recognise that unless a person is willing to engage with you, it may not be worth expending undue energy and effort. It important to make this choice only after you have made sufficient efforts to build understanding and communication.

Even in situations where it appears that we have no choice but to try and find a resolution, you do still have choices about how far you are prepared to go in order to obtain this.

Dealing with conflict

What is conflict? It is the expression of disagreement over something important to both (or all) sides of a dispute. Conflict is a natural and normal part of human life. Some of us dread it, others thrive on it. Novels and dramas depend for their interest value on situations which cause dilemmas, misunderstandings and disagreements. Working life is full of conflictual or potentially conflictual situations. The more diverse people are, the more they care about something, the greater the possibility for disagreement.

Whether or not conflict occurs in any given situation is entirely dependent on the people involved. It depends on their having a particular point of view, which may or may not have independent facts and evidence to support it, and on how they behave when they encounter an opposing point of view.

Conflict exists if at least one person believes or thinks that it exists, and engages another in the conflict process, whether the other shares the perception or not.

What are the main causes of conflict?

Conflicts of all kinds most frequently arise when people feel threatened or unjustly treated, regardless of whether the threat or treatment is real. It is harder to calm and reassure people when they are threatened or angry.

The core of human conflict is human need. When people have needs that are not being met or needs that are inconsistent with the needs of others, they engage in conflict. Conflicts arise when the people are unhappy with how they are managed or led.

The most common sources of conflict in the workplace are:

- Lack of communication about what has to be done and what is going on

- Managers who don't know what they are talking about

"The more specialist the work of the team, the more important it is that managers are perceived as being competent in that work as well as in managing."

- Managers and employees who do not do their fair share of work

- Managers who do not listen

- Unfair criticisms and accusations

- Lack of recognition and praise

- Ideas that are put into operation without evidence that they will work

- Preferential treatment

"In my experience, most conflict arises out of lack of clarity about roles, lack of boundaries, overlapping responsibilities, breakdowns in communications, either people are not communicating what they need or people bombard others with too much irrelevant information."

Handy identifies what he terms as the 'five myths that prevent conflict management'[11]:

- Conflict is a product of poor management

- Conflict is a sign of low concern for the organisation

- Anger is negative and obstructive

- Conflict, if left alone, will take care of itself
- Conflict must be responded to immediately

Conflict prevention v conflict management: anticipating conflict

Conflict can be prevented by recognising a potential source of conflict and then doing something about it before any conflict occurs.

You can anticipate and so prevent conflict by:

- Making sure that people are clear and in agreement about their role and function and about where their responsibilities begin and end

- Involving people in discussions and decisions about changes which will affect their working lives

- Taking time to communicate and not taking for granted that people have understood. See the manager as a communicator on page 33.

- Demonstrating that you are prepared to stand by your staff, if and when they are criticised. This does not mean supporting them, no matter what. It means being prepared to act as mediator and advocate in difficult situations

Working with conflict

When conflict occurs it is vital to do something about it. It is highly unlikely that conflict will simply go away unless the situation is dealt with and some resolution or agreed compromise has been reached.

However, rushing people into some sort of compromise without taking the time to look at the underlying causes of the conflict can be counter productive. People will give the appearance of having resolved the conflict when all that has happened is that it is no longer actively expressed. It is still very much there and likely to get worse and erupt at a later stage.

Conflict resolution looks at the underlying causes which started the conflict and deals with them, so that the risks of future conflict are removed or reduced. Both sides need to join together to achieve this outcome and the key to this is effective communication between all parties concerned.

Reframing conflict

Although conflict is often uncomfortable and energy-consuming, it can be a positive force for change and new learning. If you look back on your working and home life, you will probably conclude that where new ways of working were reached as a result of conflict, it was worth it, however difficult the situation was at the time.

"Someone left the department and I was expected to do the job of two people, working in two teams in two different therapeutic areas. I was extremely cross and resentful at the time and I am glad that I made my feelings known as

eventually action was taken. Six months down the line, I am realising the benefit of the new contacts I made plus the benefits of having experience in a different therapeutic area."

Over-attention to process, (remember Adair's circles on page 6) can mean that the team, or individuals within the team, lose sight of what they are there to do. Strong, firm and consistent leadership is called for where teams or individuals are unable to resolve situations. You will not please all of the people all of the time.

"My team got very stuck in backbiting and pointing fingers and blaming each other when things went wrong. I initially made the mistake of trying to appease difficult individuals by conceding to their requests. This seemed to make the situation worse. What people needed from me was fair and consistent leadership, even if they did not like it that much. Since I have stopped trying to make everyone happy and simply worked to set standards and expectations the team seems to have got back on track."

How to resolve conflicts that involve you personally
Recognise and consider the differences that exist and realise that each person involved has his or her own needs and expectations.

If you find that you are frequently in conflict with certain people, step back and try to look at things from both perspectives, your and theirs, and review why it is that this conflict keeps arising.

"I had an administrator that everyone found difficult to work with. Clients complained about her manner on the telephone and it fell to me to deal with it. I started by telling her about what strengths she brought to her work and gave her very specific examples to back my comments up. I sincerely meant these and she recognised this. I then gave her specific feedback on her telephone manner with very clear feedback on what needed to change. I then worked with her to embed the changes. She still isn't easy but she often says that I am the only one she will listen to, because I bother to acknowledge the things that do work well as well as being very clear about what needs to change and supportive about it too."

Take time to listen to the views of others, even if you do not agree with them. Encourage them to express themselves assertively. Having listened to them, request that they show the same courtesy to you, making sure that you too remain assertive rather than aggressive.

Make the effort to understand their viewpoint, even if you do not agree with it. Accept that it may be that you need to agree to differ. Recognise that it does not make either party superior if their view takes precedence or inferior if it does not.

Once the conflict has been resolved, ask yourself what you can learn from it, to make it less likely to happen in the future.

How to resolve conflicts between others when you are not personally involved

Whatever your views on the topic, and whichever of the parties you feel more sympathetic towards, it is essential to remain impartial if you are to avoid later resentment.

Some people are naturally more able to express themselves than others, so be certain to allow everyone a fair opportunity to speak.

Prevent the situation from becoming heated: all reasonable discussion, even when ideas differ, can be productive.

"One of my workers was outsourced to another company, she clashed badly with the manager there, different working styles I think. Since then, that manager has been recruited into our company and my staff member feels worried about the potential for conflict again. I pointed out that she is no longer line-managed by that person and that she has also grown in experience over the year since she has been back with us. My approach has been to support my worker without appearing to take sides, although she knows that I would be prepared to act as a mediator should there be any problems."

Things to think about before you give challenging criticism:

- *Do I have the right to criticise?*
- *Have I set standards ?*

People need to know exactly what they are expected to aim for.

- *Criticise in private*
- *Check your intentions*

Ask yourself, what is the purpose of this criticism? What am I trying achieve?

Challenging criticism needs to have a constructive purpose. Delivering it simply to blame or to crush people is counter-productive to obtaining the best performance from them.

- *Choose your manner*

Ask yourself, how are you going to speak and act? You need to prepare carefully for any tricky conversation. Your approach should be designed to make the best of a situation. While you may need to deliver difficult feedback, aim to do so in a way which does not accuse or encourage unnecessarily defensive behaviour from your staff member. While you are not responsible for anyone else's reactions, the tone you set can do much to foster an atmosphere of openness and potential willingness to engage with the issue.

- *Seek information first, you may not need to criticise*

Make sure that you are clear on the facts of the matter. If you get these wrong, you risk alienating your staff member.

Things to think about when you receive challenging criticism:

- *Ask yourself, what can I learn from this?*

There is no failure, only feedback. All feedback, whether positive or challenging is a tool for improvement. We can choose to see it as wholly negative or destructive, or we can choose to use it to the benefit of our personal and professional development. Even where you perceive criticism as wholly unjust or damaging, there are still positive lessons to extract. It may be, for example, that your experience gives you a good insight into how not to deliver feedback yourself.

- *Acknowledge your emotions*

If you feel upset, hurt or angry, remember that it is completely natural and normal to feel that way. Allow yourself the time out you need to work through your emotional responses and give a considered reaction to the feedback.

- *Check understanding*

Avoid jumping to conclusions about what you have heard or thought you heard. Take time to clarify exactly what it is that is being said to you.

- *Do something about it*

Use the feedback to inform constructively your performance.

Three main types of human behaviour

We are complex creatures, and there is a danger in labelling any individual as a particular type. Circumstances and people, bring out differing aspects of us: an individual may behave submissively in one situation, aggressively in another and act assertively in yet other areas.

"I am excellent in negotiation with investigators, I know my job and exactly what I am there to achieve. Put me a position of having to complain in a restaurant or in a shop and I give in every time."

It is worth considering the general characteristics of the three types of behaviour in order to best recognise aspects of it in ourselves and in others.

Aggressive

The person behaving aggressively operates entirely from self interest and is determined to get their own way. They tend to see situations as battles to be fought and won and they need to be the winner.

Someone who is behaving aggressively will often have a lot of energy and may well be good at what they do, but their behaviour will prevent them receiving the genuine appreciation of others. Relationships in the workplace are likely to be based on fear.

Aggressive people are usually insecure. Someone who is confident and has reasonably high self-esteem will not feel the need to win at any cost. Anyone who is sure of themselves does not have to prove their power to others.

The Institute of Clinical Research

Submissive

A person behaving submissively will always put others needs before their own, even if this is detrimental to them and even where they resent it. They are likely also to be lacking in self-confidence and insecure and this is shown in passive as opposed to aggressive behaviour.

Submissive behaviour means that a person will usually cover up what they really think and feel. Low self-esteem may mean that a submissive person is quite unable to accept compliments. They are likely to reject or literally not hear any attempts to praise. Submissive behaviour can make people a victim. A victim to circumstances and to the will and whim of others.

Passive-aggressive behaviour occurs when a person reacts internally highly aggressively but is unable to externalise this and behaves in passive or submissive ways. You often see this behaviour when someone feels powerless to change the situation in which they find themselves. They are very angry, hurt and resentful but do not feel able to challenge the circumstances giving rise to these emotions.

Assertive

An assertive person is mindful of the need for a fair balance between their rights and responsibilities and the rights and responsibilities of others. People who behave assertively do not necessarily think that everything they do is right; they are willing to accept the possibility of making mistakes. When mistakes are made, they can accept it and act to put it right. They have a positive self-image that enables them to respect themselves and others too.

The manager as coach and mentor

What is coaching?

Take a moment to consider your personal definition of coaching.

It is difficult to come up with a precise definition upon which everyone will agree. This is because people will have different views about what coaching is, what it does and how it does it.

Consider the following ideas:

Coaching is:

- bringing out the best in people
- enabling people to reach their optimum potential
- improving individual performance
- to train or teach
- to input skills and knowledge
- helping people reach their goals
- setting goals for people and giving them the skills and knowledge to reach them

You may agree with several of the above descriptions. You may favour one or two above others. Broadly speaking, how we view coaching will depend on whether or not we see it primarily as an opportunity to transfer our skills and expertise to others (input coaching), or whether we see it as an opportunity to enable people to identify issues and to find ways forward for themselves (output coaching).

Coaching is a way of enabling an individual to develop in order that they may perform at their best. Some people say that the principle behind coaching is that of seeing people in terms of what they can do in the future, not what they have done in the past.

Others have called it 'unlocking a person's potential to maximise their own performance, helping people to learn rather than teaching them.'

The object of coaching may be to reach a work-related target, to perform at a higher level more generally, or to pursue or change a career direction.

One framework for coaching
The GROW model of coaching offers a framework for thinking about what the process of coaching can address and achieve:

- Goal setting: what is your goal? The coach works with the person to establish what it is they want. The emphasis here is on creating goals or objectives, which are specific. Just as in goal setting in any performance management situation, it can be useful to follow the SMARTER model. See page 29.
- Reality check: what is your current situation? How realistic is this goal, how possible is it to attain given the person's current circumstances?
- Options: how can you reach your goal? What are your options (the more the better)?
- What action will be taken: what will you do to reach the goal? How committed are you to doing it?

Output coaching is much more about listening and questioning than about telling. The purpose is to empower the individual to learn for and by themselves, with your encouragement and support, rather than to teach. Active listening and purposeful, reflective questioning will encourage such self-development.

It is useful to develop a coaching plan with the individual concerned. This should include:

- The goals for the individual
- Timescales
- Any possible risks involved
- Some concrete success indicators

Progress can be measured against the plan during the coaching sessions.

What kind of coaching relationship works best?

The relationship that works best is one in which there is trusting, constructive communication, based on mutual respect between two adults. Coaching is best seen as 'a conversation' between peers and equals, rather than between the manager and a staff member.

Each individual is unique, people learn differently and you need to know what approach works best for them. Determining this requires that you take the time to find out what they need in order to make the most of the sessions. This requires effective questioning and listening skills.

Each situation is unique and you need flexibility. What works well in one situation may not work well in another.

Keys to successful coaching:

- Address the needs of the person you are coaching. What is important is that you address a person's needs in ways that are meaningful and relevant to them. Demonstrating your expertise is not the focus of the sessions

- You do not have to know or have all the answers

- Ask the right questions. This prompts people to reflect and think, it involves them and creates an active relationship, it also allows people to use their own insights and experience as opposed to yours

- Learn from and value failure

- Enable and encourage people to take risks: we often learn more from what goes wrong than from what went right

"I failed my way to success"   Thomas Edison

When is a need a coaching need?

You may decide to use coaching:

- As part of regular one-to-one meetings

- When delegating new tasks

- When a team member comes to you with a problem

- When a piece of work appears to be going wrong and mistakes are being made

- If a team member is looking concerned or stressed

- As part of performance reviews

- As an ongoing tool for performance management

- For more thinking on this see 'Situational Leadership' on page 19.

Coaching and mentoring: What's the difference?

"As definitions of 'mentor' tend to include all three roles, i.e. teacher, advisor, coach, I'd suggest that 'mentoring' might be more accurately described as a broad approach to supporting someone's long-term development." **Scott Welch**

What is mentoring?

Who would you describe as being a mentor to you? What is it about this person that led you to recognise them as your mentor?

The term 'mentor' is taken from a story in the Odyssey in which Odysseus entrusts the care and nurturing of his son Telemachus to his friend Mentor.

Here is one description of the mentoring process for you to consider:

"A nurturing process in which a more skilled or more experienced person, serving as a role model, teaches, encourages, counsels and befriends a less skilled or less experienced person for the purpose of promoting the latter's professional and/or personal development. Mentoring functions are carried out within the context of an ongoing, caring relationship between the mentor and mentee".

The five functions of mentoring can be described as:

- teaching
- sponsoring (protecting, supporting, promoting)
- encouraging
- counselling
- befriending

Mentoring techniques can be similar those of coaching. The difference lies in:

The nature of the relationship	More distant; not working in the same department, or at the same or immediate superior level.
The focus of discussion	Personal behaviour, relationships, career aspirations, rather than immediate work performance
Frequency of interaction	Occasional and driven by the 'mentee' rather than the mentor

When is mentoring most likely to succeed?

- When there is a need for advice and long-term personal development
- When a person is in a position to select their mentor
- When the mentor is perceived as experienced, skilled and trustworthy by the person they are mentoring
- When mentoring occurs on an occasional basis at the request of the person being mentored

The Institute of Clinical Research

Chapter Five - Leading and Managing Teams

What makes teams successful?

Think of teams that you regard as successful in the world of business, sport or entertainment? What characteristics do they have in common?

Successful teams are united by a common purpose and clear goals and objectives.

Everyone is working toward the same ends and they fully understand and embrace the goals and objectives.

Individuals know the role that they play in the team and know the value of that role. They feel accountable to other team members and recognise that by failing to play their part, they risk jeopardising the performance of the team.

Effective team work can sometimes transcend problems associated with lack of resources. Think of unsuccessful teams. Sometimes all the money and extra person power in the world cannot mend the problems caused by ineffective team working.

When do you need a team?
Quite simply, when to achieve a task, people need to work together. Think TEAM: Together Everyone Achieves More. The output of a team is greater than the sum of its parts.

Teams accomplish things that individuals working alone cannot do because the task is complex and involves input from diverse expertise.

Working together has the potential for better results and greater flexibility. Teams in which members support and encourage each other can take more risks, generate new ideas and grow in skill, confidence and commitment as individuals and as a team.

Teams v groups
Many 'teams' in the workplace are not teams but groups of people working together. Sales teams can be like this. Each member has their own individual targets. These are personal objectives and meeting these targets is not dependent on the actions of other team members. It's a team in name only and can be more accurately described as a working group.

Do teams always need leaders?
It's possible to share the leadership in very small teams. The larger the team and the more diverse and complex the tasks, the greater the need for management, direction and support. Having said this, high performing teams are capable of demonstrating high levels of self-organisation and commitment.

In the 6th century BC, Loa Tzu observed:
"But of a good leader, who talks little, when his work is done, his aim fulfilled, the people will all say, 'we did this ourselves."

Reviewing team work in your team

Team working encourages and helps teams succeed. It is a process, not a goal. Central to this process is communication. What does effective communication mean in this context? Members are enabled to share ideas and information, and co-operate and support one another in an environment that encourages openness.

Critically consider the following statements. How far do you think they are true of your team?

- Members fully understand and actively embrace common goals and objectives

- Members fully understand their own roles and the roles of other team members

- Team members take personal responsibility for their role and performance

- The team has high aspirations and standards

- Appropriate mutual support exists within the team

- Appropriate mutual trust exists within the team

- Team members communicate effectively

- Good relationships exist between the team and other parts of the organisation: the team looks outwards

- Individual professional development needs are addressed

- The team is not leader dependant, all members take their share of responsibility

- Conflict is resolved through discussion

- Mistakes are not seen in terms of blame or fault but are reviewed and learned from

- New ideas are constantly encouraged

- Team meetings are purposeful and productive

It is useful to take a leap of informed imagination and review these statements from the perspective of the most difficult member of your team.

How far would their responses accord or differ from your own?

Building Teams

"It's a complete disaster not to invest in the emotional infrastructure of your team. If they are not functioning together and interacting well together, no-one is going anywhere."

Team building is a goal, not a process. The goal is an effective, high performing team. You can use it to create new teams, review the performance of existing ones or to incorporate new people into the team. It is vital for setting the standards, expectations and working methods of the team. It can give the team a sense of direction, build and consolidate relationships, and uncover the resources, skills, strengths and gaps within the team.

"Team building has to be purposeful, otherwise people are bored and will not take it seriously. It needs to be carefully tailored. You as a team leader need to be involved in it, not just sit on the outside."

"In multi-cultural teams, you need to build a team culture which transcends any other culture. It's founded on respect and common, agreed ways of working that we put before anything else."

"The culture of a team is derived from its management style. It's possible to have a study team culture which is actually different from the company culture. You could be in a very task oriented company culture, where money and productivity is all that counts, but you could have built a team-working environment which rewards and values good will and collaboration. This can mean that people will come in on a Saturday morning to finish a job, out of loyalty to the team as opposed to any other reward."

Adair poses three sets of questions[12] that a leader needs to ask themselves throughout the process of team building, if the team is to operate at optimum level. Some of these are paraphrased below and they form a useful checklist. For Adair's team leadership theory see page 5.

Achieving the task:

- Am I clear what the tasks are?

- Am I clear what my responsibilities are?

- Are these agreed and clearly understood by my superior?

- How adequate are my resources for achieving the task?

- How far have I worked with each member to clearly define and agree targets and goals?

- Is the line of authority and accountability clear?

- What are the mechanisms for monitoring evaluation of progress towards achieving the task? How clearly are they understood by all?

- In case of my absence, who covers for me?

- How far am I leading by example?

Building and maintaining the team and developing individuals:

- Is the size of team appropriate?

- Are the right people working together? Is there a need to establish sub-teams?

- Are my attempts to involve people in decision-making and in consultation seen as genuine?

- How far do I encourage new ideas and suggestions?

- How effectively am I communicating information and keeping people up to date on plans and progress?

- How well do I advocate for, or represent the team to others?

- How useful and relevant are my support mechanisms to individuals within the team?

- How well do I acknowledge and celebrate individual and team successes?

- How constructively do I feed back and build on failures?

- Do I spend sufficient time with people, listening, developing and counselling?

- How effectively do I supervise and appraise?

- How adequate a provision is there for individual professional development and growth?

Team Cycles

When there is a major restructure, or when you first join a team, or when the team is newly formed, it is likely that the team will need to spend time working through just how it will operate and perform. Whenever there is change, it will affect team dynamics.

A four-stage cycle of development

This theory originally conceived by Bruce Tuckman[13] in the mid sixties tells us that all teams will go through a four-stage cycle of development. This is a perfectly normal process, but the eventual quality of performance of the team is dependant on how the team manages these stages.

Progress from one stage to another is not automatic and teams can get stuck at points in the cycle. Most teams experience these stages as overlapping rather than in linear sequence. There will be some storming in the forming period for example.

When a new member joins an existing team, the team changes and there may be a need to revisit the cycle. Remember that new individuals will also go through their own 'mini' cycle as they settle into your team.

Stage One: Forming

This is when the team first comes together. It is the planning stage. Formal rules and methods of working are still to be established. It is likely that people will be relatively guarded and polite with each other at this stage since few people want to be seen as difficult right from the outset.

When new people join a team, or when there is a shift in expectations for team members, it is important to recognise that the team will need to revisit this stage. The forming stage is very important since it is at this stage that systems, expectations and standards are discussed, debated and set. If sufficient time and attention is not paid here, then the team is likely to operate dysfunctionally.

Your role as a manager:

People will look to you, as a manager, for direction and leadership. They will expect you to convey the purpose and vision for the team and translate these into concrete goals and objectives which can be discussed and agreed. Your task here is to team build. To establish how the team will work, create communication systems, and involve members in creating these working practises. At this stage, you can identify skills and experience within the team, establish and agree roles and functions.

It helps to use your experience in other teams, either as manager or as member. What has worked well before? Preparation for these early team meetings is vital. If you are not clear about what you are trying to achieve, then no one else will be. Your team is your resource. The more you involve them in establishing working practices, the more people will own them. Before the team starts to work together, make it your job to know: what you want, what people already know and what people expect, what experience and expectations they bring to the team.

How long does the forming process take?

The length of the forming process is entirely dependent on the complexity and clarity of the task. If the team is engaged in a simple, clearly defined task, the team will spend no more than ten per cent of it's time in the forming stage. Complex and ambiguous tasks may mean that the team spends up to seventy per cent of its time in this stage.

Stage two: Storming

This marks the end of any 'honeymoon period.' You can expect upsets and ructions when people start testing each other out and clashing. This is when reality sets in and people can get quite upset. Personal agendas come to the fore, people can feel demotivated or want to opt out. There will be emotive opinions about personalities and work methods.

The Institute of Clinical Research

Your role as a manager:

Recognise and accept that people will question and challenge your leadership. This is the point at which you find out just who thinks that they could do the job better than you. It is important to anticipate difficulty, be proactive and invite challenges assertively. Avoid defensiveness. Watch out for signs of conflict and deal with issues as they arise. Consistency, flexibility and the ability to manage your own reactions are key.

Above all, recognise this as part of the normal process of team development. What's important is not the storm itself but how you manage it.

Stage three: Norming

The team starts to settle and 'norms' of behaviour, both good and poor start to emerge.

A good norm might be that the team has developed successful systems for communication. A poor norm could be that the team develops a culture of never quite meeting targets. The quality of norms that develop is dependent on how effectively stages one and two have been managed.

Your role as a manager:

It is at this point that the concept of shared responsibility and mutual accountability is firmly embedded in the working culture. You can do this by resisting the temptation to solve all of these problems yourself, or carry the team. Be open to new ideas and new ways of doing things. It may well be that some of the working methods formulated at the beginning need adaptation and modification.

Stage Four: Performing

The team produces results. The quality of these results or outputs is entirely dependant on how effectively the team has been managed through the developmental cycle.

Successful teams: pitfalls to avoid

- Resist resting on your laurels or becoming complacent as performance will slide downwards

- Avoid becoming too insular or closing ranks. Good teams look outwards

- Over-confidence and a sense of invincibility will usually mean a team stops questioning itself, learning and developing

- Teams in which everyone 'thinks the same way' can miss out on a valuable alternative perspective. Diversity and differing opinions can be very stimulating within teams just as long as they are properly addressed and worked with

Chapter Six - Working with Change

What is change?

Change, in its simplest form, can be described as 'to alter or make different.' Change is an ever present ongoing process in nearly all aspects of our lives. Particularly so, it can seem, in the world of work.

What precipitates workplace change? Here are just a few examples:

New acquisitions, mergers, changes in legislation, development and introduction of IT systems; the need to respond to clients and customers, to stay ahead of competition, to become faster, more effective and more efficient; the drive to do more with less, to research and develop more effective products; changes in staff, changes in management. All of these things engender change.

Some changes we welcome. Others we find unsettling. Why is change so unsettling? Because it brings with it uncertainty. Because the process of change is often fraught with insecurity. No one can be completely certain what the outcome will be, whether the change will be successfully realised or successfully executed.

In any complex change process, there comes a point at which one has to let go of old ways of doing things without being clear that the new ways will work.

"If you want to set sail for a distant land you have to lose sight of the shore."

André Gide

"In a time of change, leadership becomes important, leadership is the ability to inspire people to share your vision and join you in a journey."

"The more difficult the changes going on, the more people need to gain from their managers the feeling that there is a plan, that the plan is known and mostly stuck to."

Change in the workplace

Our experience of change in the workplace is dependent on many factors.

These include:

• Whether or not we played a part in choosing the change or planning for the change. Was it imposed on us? How far do we own or agree to the change?

John Harvey-Jones[14] observes:

"Organisations only change when the people in them change, and people will only change when they accept in their hearts that change must occur. Change is a 'hearts and minds' job and the engines of change are dissatisfaction with, and

fear of, maintaining the status quo. It is very difficult indeed to change against the grain of the belief of your people..."

- The level of responsibility, resources and support we have to drive the change forward

- How effectively we think that the change is being carried out

- Our hopes and fears about the consequences of the change

- How effectively we can manage the ambiguity and uncertainty inherent in the change process for ourselves and for the people that we manage

Different types of organisational change
It is helpful to consider some of the different types of changes that occur in organisations. While reading, think about changes in your organisation and where they might fit into these categories.

Planned change
Change, that is deliberate, a product of conscious reasoning and actions.

Emergent change
Emergent change is unforeseen, unplanned change or unexpected change. External factors such as the economy, politics and competitors' behaviour can have a sudden impact and force change, which is outside the control of managers and was not necessarily planned or anticipated by them.

"The new European Clinical Trials Directive has radically altered the way in which we work, we have had to write new SOPs, new trial management documentation and even create new jobs."

"As a result of unexpected serious adverse events, our study closed overnight. One minute we were working on a hayfever drug, the next on a drug in an entirely different therapeutic area."

Internal factors such as unexpected staff reaction to planned change can result in the original plan being changed and a different course of action being adopted.

"The original plan when the two companies merged was to make the CRA function an entirely field-based one across the UK. My company used office-based CRAs and they were a really strong and talented force. We strenuously objected to the plans as we all lived in the South. The new company could not afford to lose our skills and expertise, so the plan was modified to a gradual phasing out over a five-year period."

Even the most carefully planned and executed change programme will have some emergent impacts. In other words, no matter how hard we try to plan, there will always be something that we haven't foreseen.

Episodic change

Episodic change is planned change, which occurs infrequently and has a clear start and end point. The introduction of new software is an example of episodic change.

"Our company introduced new project software, this has impacted on our roles as clinical trial administrators and demanded the acquisition of new skills and differing job responsibilities. We initially found the idea very worrying and resisted changes to our roles, but throughout the process we have been included in conversations about the need and benefits of the new system. The company has invested time and money in offering training and support and has given us the opportunity to restructure the roles in a way which we see could work. We have felt listened to and valued, even senior management has bothered to come and speak with us. What could have been a very difficult change process has been made far easier by the way in which it has been handled."

Continuous Change

Continuous change is change, that is ongoing. Continuous change is characterised by people constantly adapting, modifying and altering, accepting change as part of the everyday reality of working life. It could be argued that, if we recognise change is always with us and is inevitable, then we have a realistic approach to working life and life outside work. However, we all know what it is like to feel that we are subject to 'too much change'. This is when the balance between stability and security and change feels unequal.

Developmental, transitional and transformative change

Developmental change may be either planned or emergent. It is usually concerned with acquiring or improving skills. Examples of this are learning to drive or learning to use a new software programme.

"Our global organisation decided that all trials will be managed according to a new Electronic Trial Management System and this has to be rolled out across the world. This means that not only do we have to become familiar with the new system, it also has knock-on effects on how we deal with emails and phone calls."

The above change gives rise to developmental training needs at three levels: organisational, occupational and individual. The whole company is affected as are the job functions within the company and individuals within those functional areas.

Transitional change is concerned with the movement from one state to another. It is episodic and planned. The example above is also an example of transitional change.

In the early 20th century, psychologist Kurt Lewin developed a three-stage process to describe this sort of change:

1. Unfreezing

2. Moving

3. Refreezing

Unfreezing involves letting go of the existing structure. In the above example, existing trial management systems are shelved. Moving is quite literally the movement between the old ways of doing things and the new ways. Refreezing is what happens when people have moved into the new roles and new ways of working.

Transformational Change
This is complete change. When an organisation completely changes or transforms itself and becomes significantly different to what it was before.

"As a small training provider in the field of conflict resolution, we have recently undergone a strategic review and have redefined ourselves as a research-based organisation, looking at new ways of managing conflict. Our focus will no longer be on delivering conflict resolution programmes but on undertaking cutting edge research in this area."

Your personal perceptions of change
Looking back over the last twelve months, consider any significant changes that you have been involved with at work. Select two examples of change, think about which type of change these represent and analyse your reactions and actions. Use the following questions to guide your analysis:

- What were the main implications of the change? Where they positive or negative?

- What were the unforeseen implications of the change, if any?

- How did the change affect your behaviour/thinking/attitudes? Why?

- How did the change make you feel?

- Did you feel in control of the change?

- Did the change impact on other people? If so how was this managed?

- How would you rate your decision-making skills with regard to the change? Could they have been improved? If so, how?

- On reflection, what would you have done differently?

What makes us resist or avoid change?

John Hagel of McKinseys observed:

"Change is threatening. It means doing things differently, perhaps in ways that an individual will not be able to master. Change is difficult. It is always easier to continue to do things the same comfortable way rather than trying something new. Change is risky. If the new methods don't work, or if people lose sight of immediate needs while trying to master them, near-term performance may suffer, perhaps disastrously. Change is often illusory. Too many organisations have grown cynical as senior management announces yet another change initiative that will fall by the wayside three or four months later when some new issue diverts attention elsewhere."[15]

Managing resistance to change

Understanding your own responses

As a manager of any change process, you need to be clear about your own responses to the change. How far have you bought into the need for change? How ambivalent are you about the process? What do you see as the obstacles inherent within the process and how are you working with these obstacles?

There are times when you may not see the point and purpose of the proposed changes. Your responsibility here is to find a way of approaching this as constructively as possible. You can be transparent with staff about your own reservations at the same time as requesting that as a team or department you collaboratively find a way of making the best of it.

"In a recent systems and process audit which did not directly concern me or my team, I had to persuade several of the team to help out with preparing archives and reviewing SOPs simply because these things had not been done correctly in the first place. This meant that people had to quite literally drop what they were doing and they were already very busy. It seemed to me that the reputation of the company was at stake. I needed put aside my own objectives for a while and I needed to work with my team to persuade them to do the same, even though we all felt that this could and should not have been necessary."

Working with the responses of others

A manager should recognize that every change creates some inevitable resistance and be open to the possibility of it emerging at any stage in the change process. Plans for change should include strategies around working with resistance.

It makes sense to see resistance as a potential tool for learning as opposed to an unwelcome and threatening obstacle. Negative responses can lead to constructive information about the change if handled appropriately. You could learn something, which will improve the change process.

Carol O'Connor observes:

"Some managers react forcefully to resistance. Their aim is to control it, stop it, negate it, in short, make it go away. This response doesn't work because it resists resistance. It is a defensive reaction to a defensive action. It creates two entrenched and resistant positions, not just one, with neither side willing to give way to the other."

Those who resist plans for change may in fact have different definitions of the problem or beliefs about its seriousness. While they may say aloud that: 'This plan won't work', they may actually be thinking: 'This plan doesn't address the real issue'. Only through discussion can mutual understanding be developed.

To resolve resistance, a manager must willingly explore what causes it. There is no other way. Acknowledging contradiction and criticism can seem like playing into the hands of the opposition. This is where both self-awareness and a sense of humour bring most benefit. Managers with a balanced and fair perspective and the ability to maintain a 'light touch' are always in control. This is because for them 'control' includes the idea that other people can have different points of view. Managers control change by coordinating these differences into an integrated whole and by allowing colleagues to contribute their positive and negative views[16].

Responses to change
In any given population, people will respond to change in one of five ways:

This is a reductive way of looking at things but is useful in terms of allowing us to see the complex reactions to change within a framework of five main responses.

1. Champions   10% of the population
   Those who are right behind the change. who agree with it and actively embrace it

2. Chasers   15% of the population
   Those who are open minded to the possibility of the change, but who want to hear more before they make the decision to actively embrace it

3. Converts   50% of the population
   The majority, who will wait to see how things are shaping up before they make a decision either way

4. Challengers   15% of the population
   Those who have active reservations about the changes and who need to have this addressed, otherwise they will not support the change

5. Change-a-phobics   10% of the population
   Those who are utterly close-minded to the change and no amount of persuasion will move them from this position

The Institute of Clinical Research

Where we sit in this spectrum will depend on a complex mix of personal reactions to change in general and responses to a particular and specific set of changes. It's very possible to be a chaser in one arena and a challenger in another. Just as there are a few of us who will resist any type of change, and there are others who, more often than not make ready champions of change.

How to manage the change process
As a manager, you will be dealing with a diverse set of responses within your team to any change process.

Question: Which of the five responses to change do you most need to address in order for the change process to have the best chance of success?

Answer: The challengers. Why? Because if you cannot get these people on board, then you will find that they will impact negatively on the decision of your converts.

Your next most urgent group are the chasers. They need to know more before they will actively agree and so bring the converts along with them.

Many managers make the mistake of focusing on the change-a-phobic. This is somewhat like the proverbial beating of one's head against a brick wall. Remember that you cannot change anyone, they can only change themselves. Concentrating on closed-minded individuals is a waste of your time.

Never stop communicating
This applies even when you have no news. In situations where people feel threatened, uncertain and insecure, they need to be kept up to date. This can sometimes mean explaining that you do not yet know what the next steps are or that strategies and plans are not yet clear. It's a common mistake made by managers to stay silent unless they have something concrete to say. The consequence of this is that rumours abound. Where there is silence, people will 'fill the gap' and posit all sorts of plans and schemes that are being 'secretly enacted above their heads'.

You have the difficult task of creating a sense of transparency throughout the change process. This means being honest about what you do or do not know. There will be times when you have information that you are not at liberty to divulge. You will need to be as transparent as possible about this, explaining why and remaining consistent and non-defensive in your approach.

Questions your team will want addressed
You will need to prepare yourself to provide satisfactory answers to some fundamental queries from staff.

These may include:

- Will my job description change?
- Will I lose my job?
- How long will all this take?
- What exactly is happening and why is it happening?
- What do I have to do?
- What will I stand to lose or gain from it?
- What are the benefits to us as a team? To us as an organisation?
- Does this mean I am going to end up with more work?

Conclusion

This monograph has taken you through some of the key issues involved in people management. People management is a messy business, it can be hard work and certainly it is difficult to get 'right'.

Effective management starts with you managing you. The best managers are willing to critically consider their strengths and limitations and areas for development. Good managers recognise that while they may not get it right all the time, they can learn from their mistakes.

The best people managers are those who are genuinely interested in the professional development of the people that they manage and who act on the belief that people are likely to perform at their best when they are trusted, supported and empowered.

Effective managers realise that people management is not synonymous with caring and support. The ability to take tough decisions, to challenge, stimulate, inspire, provide focus, set expectations and standards, direct, coach and delegate where and as appropriate are just as important. They expect the best from people and are also prepared to deal with and find ways to work through areas of difficulty.

Mastering the art of management is probably a lifelong learning process. I hope this monograph will have been of some use on that journey.

References

1. *Thomas, N.,* The John Adair Handbook of Management and Leadership, p125, Thorogood, 2004

2. *Thomas, N.,* The John Adair Handbook of Management and Leadership, pp118-126, Thorogood, 2004

3. *Tan, J.H.,* Management Work in Singapore: Developing a Factor Model, Henley Management College/Brunel University,1994

4. *Thomas, N.,* The John Adair Handbook of Management and Leadership, p126, Thorogood, 2004

5. *Goleman, D.,* The Harvard Business Review, Article 98606, Nov/Dec1998

6. *Peters, T.M,* The Brand Called You, Fast Company, Aug/Sept 1997

7. *Thomas, N.,* The John Adair Handbook of Management and Leadership, p5, Thorogood, 2004

8. *Blanchard, K., Zigarmi, P., Zigarmi, D.,* Leadership and the One Minute Manager, HarperCollins Business, 1994

9. *Schon, D.,* The Reflective Practitioner: How Professionals Think in Action, Basic Books,1983

10. *McGregor, D.,* The Human Side of Enterprise, McGraw-Hill, New York 1985

11. *Handy, C.,* The Age of Unreason, Harvard Business School Press, 1989

12. *Thomas, N.,* The John Adair Handbook of Management and Leadership, p146, Thorogood, 2004

13. *Tuckman, B.,* Developmental Sequence in Small Groups, Pyschological Bulletin, 63; 1965

14. *Harvey-Jones, J.,* Managing to Survive, Heineman, 1993

15. *Hagel, J.,* Keeping CPR on Track, McKinsey Quarterly, May 1993

16. *O'Connor, C.A.,* Chapter 7, The Handbook for Organisational Change, McGraw Hill, 1993

Bibliography

The following books provide useful overviews of:

Management thinking:
Crainer, S., **Key Management Ideas,** 3rd Edition, Prentice Hall, 1998

Thomas, N., **The John Adair Handbook of Management and Leadership,** Thorogood, 2004

Kennedy, C., **Managing with the Gurus,** Century, 1996

Topping, P., **Managerial Leadership,** MCGraw Hill, 2002

Situational leadership:
Blanchard, K., **Leadership and the One Minute Manager,** HarperCollins,1994

New thinking in management:
Battram, A., **Navigating Complexity,** The Industrial Society, 2001

Stacey, R., Griffin, D., Shaw, P., **Complexity and Management,** Routledge, 2002

The Institute of Clinical Research

Maria Henderson Library
Gartnavel Royal Hospital
Glasgow G12 0XH Scotland